MW01633683

Horst Rechelbacher is a passionate visionary whose ideals have shaped the lives of so many.

William P. Lauder
President and CEO, The Estée Lauder Companies

Alivelihood is a profound reminder of ancient truths, presented in the most engaging compassionate style, calling on the reader to look at the difference between what we know and what we truly use! Horst's insights have inspired me to go higher in my walk for peace, joy, and wisdom.

Vivienne Mackinder
Former Artistic Director, Vidal Sassoon and Trevor Sorbie, Movie Director, Producer

Horst is a visionary who shares the holistic view of reality which is transforming the world today. I have read his brilliant book twice now. Beyond Horst's inspiring life story is so much wisdom for the global mind-change that I will keep his book handy and refer to it often.

Candace B. Pert, Ph.D.
Author of "Molecules of Emotion", Neuroscientist

When you read this book, you will understand why Horst inspired and touched so many individuals.

Dominique Conseil
President, Aveda Corporation

Printed with soy inks, on old growth forest free 100% recycled paper

ALIVELIHOOD

The Art of Sustainable Success

By Horst M. Rechelbacher

Founder of Aveda and Intelligent Nutrients

With Victor J. Zurbel & Ellen Daly

HMR PUBLISHING
1017 Cascade Street
Osceola, WI 54020
(715) 294-1808
info@hmrpublishing.com
www.hmrpublishing.com

ALIVELIHOOD...THE ART OF SUSTAINABLE SUCCESS

The values and principles that I share
in this book have come to me from many teachings.
They are what I try my best to practice
and they continue to evolve, as do the lessons of life.
Therefore, I am still a student.

I dedicate this book to all my teachers—
past, present, and future.

HORST M. RECHELBACHER

Contents

PREFACE

The Merriam-Webster Dictionary defines success as: the attainment of wealth, favor, or eminence. The *Alivelihood* model of success is defined by a whole different value system: it is measured by how well our personal life mission aligns with our corporate or business mission and how well that aligns with our earth's mission, which is the sustainability and continuation of all life.

This is future-minded thinking. When our mission of success includes future generations, it can guide us to make the right choices for both today and tomorrow. It can guide us through our current state of planetary crisis and allow us to see the great opportunities of our moment. It can give us the vision to create products and services that support a sustainable future and to fulfill our personal needs while making a difference in the world.

Whether you're an entrepreneur, a corporate employee, or a CEO, you can make a difference by transforming yourself and contributing to the health and well-being, other people and our planet. You can help to create a business and a workplace based on ethics, trust, and respect, and attain the true success that comes from aligning every aspect of your life with the purpose of life itself.

In *Alivelihood*, Horst Rechelbacher shares the principles and practices he has learned and applied in over thirty-five years as an "ecopreneur." Horst invites you to partner with him and other visionary businesspeople to create a new era of "enlightened capitalism," turning the industrial revolution into "the sustainable evolution."

It's a great challenge, but what could be more important when our planet's Alivelihood is at stake?

Victor J. Zurbel, 2005

INTRODUCTION:

THE BUSINESS OF LIFE

There are many books on business success and many others on self-improvement, but my philosophy and experience is that both subjects are interrelated. Every approach to self-improvement requires some form of internal and external negotiation, and in all of our interactions with others, there is some form of business transaction.

As an Austrian, I interpret the word *business* from the German language, which in English can be translated as *trans-action*, or the exchange of action. The word *action* can also be interpreted to mean *energy*, your energy and my energy, so we could say that business is, in essence, the exchange of energy.

Looking at it this way, we are all in business, both inwardly and outwardly. Some trade cash, stocks, or bonds, while others trade services, commodities, real estate, art, or intellectual property. In our inner world, we trade thoughts, feelings, actions, and information. If we were to observe all the inner transactions we conduct on a daily basis, we would be amazed to discover the many unconscious ways we do business in this regard.

By interpreting business as an exchange of energy, we can also observe that all of biological life works as a business enterprise. Take plants, for example. Through the process of photosynthesis, plants absorb energy from the sun and convert carbon dioxide into oxygen. Hence, they use their energy to support other biological life, which reciprocates by using its energy to support plant life. But unfortunately, we *Homo sapiens* are no longer operating in this way; on the contrary, we are destroying our plant life by deforestation and clear-cutting. We are squandering our planet's energy, especially the energy we derive from oil and petrochemicals, and in the process setting in motion unnatural cycles that threaten to destroy life on earth.

Before it's too late, we must become aware that all the elements of our planet are in business together for the purpose of sustainability. We are not having honest and healthy business transactions with our planetary corporation, Earth, Inc., and the way we do "business" with the earth is symptomatic of the greedy, self-serving way we do business on the stock exchange, as well as the fear-driven, unconscious way we do business with ourselves.

It's time to make holistic, sustainable values an imperative in our lifestyles and our corporations' policies. We have a great responsibility not just to our corporate shareholders but also to our planetary shareholders—to all living beings and to future generations. My companies have been founded on a single principle: that humans are interconnected with all of life. This is what I mean when I use the term "holistic"—it means that which takes into account all the interdependent elements of life. Let us learn to do business holistically—both inwardly and outwardly—and bring a fair and honest exchange of actions back into all of our trans-actions.

My approach to "alivelihood" starts with I, Inc.—the art of managing our personal lives as if we were each a corporation. We should strive to become CEOs of our thoughts, emotions, and sensory impressions. Instead of allowing them to take over the "business of being," which they normally do, we can make them our partners and work together with a unified vision and mission in service of others and the Earth. Then we can take the next step and form a merger—we can merge I, Inc. with We, Inc., and create a holistic business built on the values of personal responsibility, teamwork, and interdependency. Finally, we can work together with other organizations to make Earth, Inc. a successful and sustainable planet.

Once we understand the complex interconnectedness of mind, body, and spirit; the relationship between our actions and our senses; the association between ourselves and others in our lives; and the inescapable links between past, present, and future; we will begin to build a truly holistic lifestyle. Through awakening to the fact that all of life is in business together, and ultimately works together or fails together, we can become "eco-preneurs" and "eco-consumers"- creative partners in our own and our planet's alivelihood.

Part I:

I, Inc. - The Business of Being

"The more deeply I search

for the roots of our global environmental crisis,

the more I am convinced that it is

an outer manifestation of an inner crisis that is,

for lack of a better word, spiritual."

–Al Gore

Vice President

Earth in the Balance

Minding our own Business

The first question we should ask ourselves before endeavoring to create a successful, sustainable lifestyle or business venture is: are we creating success in our inner business? We are rarely conscious of what is going on inside us, so it is little wonder we have created such a mess in the world around us. In order for humanity to bring about a nurturing, environmentally aware and sustainable new future, each one of us as individuals needs to wake up, to become conscious of our inner transactions and the cycles of cause and effect that make us interdependent with all of life. By bringing mindfulness to our daily thoughts and actions, we will be building a foundation for our inner and outer businesses to thrive, rather than just survive. The art of sustainable success begins, therefore, with minding our own business.

We may think that simply because we have our eyes open, we are awake. And on a certain level, we are. But are we really, consciously awake, open to all the realities of life? Are we aware of the pace of our own breath, of the fragrances and sounds that surround us? How often do we stop to actually taste our food as we're eating it? Are we aware of our goals—for the day, for the week, for the year, for this lifetime—and of how each moment affects our achievement of them? Are we aware of how our actions and achievements impact the world around us? Are we aware of what the planet needs to support future generations?

In modern life, it is all too common for us to go through our days half asleep. There are so many impulses that tempt us to check out, mentally, emotionally, and spiritually, from our own experiences. Distraction is everywhere—on the television, on the internet, at the shopping mall. And constant distraction dulls our senses, which are vital tools for our development. When we use distractions to suppress uncomfortable emotions such as stress, anger, fear, and jealousy, those feelings will inevitably color how we are and how we interact and trans-act with others. They may even manifest themselves as physical ailments. Only through awareness can we avoid this dis-ease and not spread it into the world around us. If we are willing to be awake and conscious, we will find that we can adjust and improve many of the subconscious relationships we carry on within our internal and external worlds.

The quick-fix solutions many people seek are often the result of an unwillingness to be present and conscious in life. The suppression of emotional pain has become a huge business, with billions of dollars being spent on prescription drugs and recreational drugs and myriad other forms of escape. But experiencing pain is a natural part of life. In fact, it is a teacher, because it can alert us to something that needs our attention. Pain can be seen as a message from our true self—a request for consciousness!

If we learn to analyze the *causes* of pain without judging, without making it right or wrong, we will find that it is a profound stimulus for healing. I personally believe that God does not judge—God only offers love. Judging is a human invention that we have adopted to control each other. I make every effort not to use the words "right" and "wrong." Instead, I ask myself, "Is this action creating pain or bliss?" If the answer is bliss, then I know I'm on the right track; if it's pain, then I realize it's time to become more conscious.

Judgment of others is usually a result of fear in the mind. All the feelings we try so hard to avoid—pain, envy, jealousy, violence, revenge, mistrust, depression, and anger—are rooted in fear. Fear is the largest blocker of all systems and a huge cause of stress, emotional and physical. Indeed, the majority of us live in constant subliminal fear. Why? Due to lack of self-observation. It's our habit to avoid and deny fear, but this only feeds it. Our fear of fear itself is self-perpetuating. The only way to heal fear is to become conscious of it, to study its cause and effect.

Fear is a reaction to previous sensory impressions—to the abusive, traumatic and terrifying experiences we have all been through, which are permanently stored in the mind. The mind-field is a dangerous place to be stumbling through half asleep! We all have explosives embedded in our nervous systems—in my own case, almost literally. I was born in Austria in 1941, and one of my earliest memories is from the age of four, when the Allies bombed the railroad station in our beautiful lakeside town and a stray bomb hit the house right opposite ours. My mother, brother and I fled to the basement in terror. The fear generated by that event is living in me to this day and I empathize with children all over the world who are subjected to the horrors of war. We all relive our personal fears along with today's global terror and violence, and our media tends to fuel this, constantly recycling impressions of our violent history as it reports on current events.

In the midst of fear, thinking clearly is very difficult because the mind speeds up. Being conscious in this state is a skill few of us possess. We need to learn to identify the cause of the fear or pain and surrender to it. We cannot fight the cause, since it has already happened, but we can heal the pain by not repeating the cause in our own responses to others. The most important tool to fight fear, pain, or anger is not judgment, blame or revenge, but surrender and forgiveness. This is not cowardice or weakness; it's intuitive intelligence, and it takes great courage. The antidote for fear is courage—the courage to practice selflessness, compassion, and forgiveness.

I learned my first lesson in compassion from my relationship with my father. He had fought in the Second World War, and was held in a Russian prison camp for two years afterwards. I remember him as a quiet man who worked hard making custom shoes for people who had crippled feet, of whom there were many in postwar Austria, and also for athletes and well-to-do clients. Although his business was successful, he partied and got drunk every Saturday night until all the money he had worked so hard for the entire week was gone. When he finally came home, my mother would confront him, and it always ended up in a fight with physical abuse. I was the only one to witness this ordeal; my two older brothers had already left home. Mother never complained, and this made me very angry. However, I later learned that my father had been tortured in the prison camp and severely abused as a child by the headmaster of his orphanage. Hence, he was a victim of abuse who became an abuser himself when he was drunk. When I understood this, I was able to forgive him.

One of the keys to true success in life is the ability to forgive and generate compassion for others. Holding on to resentments blocks our flow of energy and creates a tremendous amount of inner stress and dis-ease, so although we may attain success in the world outside, we will not experience it within ourselves. If another person is the cause of our emotional pain, it is because they are experiencing pain within themselves. When we try to understand what another's needs are and serve them, we are bringing healing and happiness to the whole situation—theirs and ours. As His Holiness the Dalai Lama, one of the greatest living examples of compassion, has said: "If you want others to be happy, practice compassion. If you want to be happy, practice compassion."

The Art of Service

Service is often given lower class status, but I consider it a healing art. Not only is good service the key to a successful, sustainable business; it is also, as many of the ancient traditions tell us, a practice that is essential for spiritual development.

Business can provide us with an opportunity to do more than enrich ourselves; it can provide us with an opportunity to serve. We can enrich others with products and services that are healthy and non-toxic, that make them feel good and improve the quality of their life. When I am doing business, I also consider what other people's needs are from a holistic and sustainable point of view and I take those into account in the products and services I offer. That way, I'm not just serving my customers as individual, separate units, but honoring and serving them in their relationship to the earth. This kind of respect is what I consider true customer service.

In Austria, where I grew up, the art of service was ingrained in the old world European culture. Showing respect and good manners to the many Barons, Baronesses and government bureaucrats was an absolute requirement, and I consider myself lucky to have been taught the value of service and diplomacy so early in life.

As a young man, I had part-time jobs after school in a delicatessen and a hairdressing salon. The owner of the delicatessen was a kind, older man who taught me the art of displaying his products, which were freshly prepared with produce from the local farmers. Several times a week, the head chef of the Baroness von Hollenburg came to shop with his entourage of assistants. He had a reputation as a great chef, but he was fussy and arrogant. In those days, everything was displayed on plates, as there was no packaging. My boss instructed me that if the chef was to reject a butter, cheese, meat, or any other food, and we had no substitute, I was to take it to the back room, re-cut or reshape it and bring it back out to the chef to smell and taste. To my amazement, the chef almost always thought the "new" food was much better, and my boss had a twinkle in his eye after the exchange. It was a true lesson in the principle that "the customer is always right."

I am surprised how few of us believe in this principle today. We find it difficult to admit we could have been of better service. We take life too personally, protecting ourselves first, and therefore are unable to feel the other person's pain because of our fear-based mentality. We are afraid of being wrong, afraid of losing face. But who loses then? Unfortunately, both. Both experience stress and anger, and the customer loses now and the business loses later.

If we can create a formula for true customer service in our lifestyles and our businesses, there is no way we can lose. Success, in this paradigm, is measured not by dollars, but by endorphins—the body's natural prescription for pain relief and bliss. Scientists such as Dr. Candace Pert, a neuroscientist from Georgetown University and author of *Molecules of Emotion*, are able to scientifically document the effects of emotions on the health of cells. They have discovered that when we experience feelings of satisfaction, contentment, and being nurtured, our bodies make endorphins. These beneficial chemicals energize the body's cellular structure, making us feel good, and more importantly, they program the function of neuropeptides, which are the building blocks of our immune system. When we nurture someone else selflessly, he or she produces endorphins, and we seem to share the benefits, as our bodies produce endorphins also. But when we develop feelings of dissatisfaction, fear, loneliness, and depression, our bodies stop the production of these medicinal, beneficial chemicals, creating an unproductive and unhealthy inner environment and depressing our immune system. So when our customers are nurtured by our service and satisfied with what we have provided, it yields dividends in happiness, well-being, peace, and contentment both for them and for ourselves.

It is from my own experience with my customers that I have learned how true this is: when we give, we get; and when we don't give, we don't get. We are all customers, and we have the right to buy what we want, what we need, and what we love. When we put ourselves in the customer's shoes, we are always right. If we can serve our customers as ourselves, we create bliss for them, which can heal the pain they may be experiencing as a result of not getting what they need. Creating bliss for the "other side of ourselves" is the best way to build a relationship that is sustainable, based on honor and respect.

Despite their airs, the Austrians had great respect for each other. As a child, I was impressed by how they greeted each other on the boulevard. Men lifted their hats, smiled, and bowed their heads as they passed each other, and when meeting a woman, gallantly kissed her hand. These were not just gestures of politeness; they were genuine expressions of honor and respect. Two decades later, in Japan and India, I saw the same thing. The Japanese bow in greeting, and have perfected the art of listening to one another. The Indians fold their hands in front of their hearts in a prayer position, bow, and say, "*namaste,*" which means, "I honor the divinity within you, which is also in me." That is the spiritual way of looking at customer service: bowing to the divinity in the customer.

One of my passions is to collect and sell indigenous and religious antique artifacts. I once received a call from a New York City dealer telling me about a rare Ming Dynasty Buddha available at a very good price. He said he would send it to me with no obligations. When the package arrived, I opened it anxiously—and was somewhat taken aback. This Buddha was giving me the middle finger! I thought my dealer friend must have played a joke on me. I took the Buddha to a Chinese antique expert, who examined it, and to my surprise, told me that it was very special, and definitely authentic. What about the middle finger? I asked him. He explained that the middle finger means Oneness—it symbolizes God, who is one with everything. This Buddha now has a very special place in my house. It reminds me that when someone gives me the middle finger I must bow and see God in that person.

The Sanskrit word *seva,* which means selfless service, also means that we see ourselves in the other, and by serving them we are serving ourselves. I recently read an article describing how one five-star hotel in Bangkok sends its staff to the nearby Buddhist monastery to learn never to say no and always to think of others. I'm sure it is contributing greatly to their success. I believe that if we all learned to serve like monks, or if we operated as if we were all each other's customers, it would create miracles—not only in business, but also in our personal lives as well as our relationships with our global family. When we serve without expectation of reward, everyone gains.

THE POWER OF VISUALIZATION

Everything in the realm of manifestation begins with a desire, an idea, an intent, and a mission. We first need to want to create something and then cultivate that desire into a passion. In my experience, all the rules of success and management won't help unless we have the desire, passion and love for what we are trying to achieve. We can also call it "want-power," "need-power" or "love-power." If we *want* something enough, then we will create the will-power to go after it.

How do we create want-power? We can't just think it; we need to *feel* it. If our approach is merely intellectual, it is not likely to succeed; it must come from the heart. By visualizing our goals and feeling how wonderful it would be to manifest them, we keep the desire and passion strong. Many people make "to do" lists and plan their actions every day, but how many of us take the time to re-visualize and renew our desire, passion and love for what we want to attain?

I discovered the power of intention and visualization as a teenager. It was not something I was taught—in fact, my school years were a difficult and humiliating time that left me with little self-esteem or confidence in my own abilities. Although I was smart and creative, my grades were always low. I would later discover that I was dyslexic, but in those days neither I nor my teachers understood this, so I just felt stupid, living in constant fear of the public humiliation that usually resulted from my poor exam results. I even developed a method of avoiding school, especially at exam time—I made myself sick. At first, I faked it, fooling my mother by rubbing the thermometer between my thumb and forefinger. But after she got wise to that trick, I subconsciously developed a psychosomatic ability to actually give myself a temperature.

Eventually, my teacher suggested that since I showed little academic aptitude, I might do better in an apprenticeship program than in college. I already knew what I wanted to do: I had been looking through the window of a salon across the street from my house, impressed by the expertise of the stylists and the obvious satisfaction of the customers. At the young age of twelve, I decided I was going to become a famous and successful hair stylist.

My apprenticeship began at the age of fourteen, and soon after, I was preparing to compete in my first Austrian Junior Championship. Although I took it very seriously, staying late in the evening to practice, my technique was lacking and I was afraid I was destined for humiliation once again. With only two weeks to go before the competition, my body pulled out its old trick: I developed a high fever with tonsillitis and a kidney infection and had to be rushed to the hospital.

I was discharged a week before the competition and went straight to the salon to practice. But my technique was still weak, and my boss told me to go home and rest and wait until the following year's competition. I was determined to succeed and pleaded with him until he reluctantly conceded. I went home, but instead of resting, for the next six hours I rehearsed everything in my mind. I visualized how the hair would look and how I would style it. I saw the whole process step-by-step and felt it as vividly as if I had actually done it in person.

What was unusual, however, was that I saw the process *in reverse*. I first saw the hairstyle completed and then visualized the steps backwards all the way to the first pin curl. That night, I went outside and looked up at the starry sky. I picked a star to make a wish on. But then I did an interesting thing: since I was now already confident, instead of wishing on the star, I thanked it in advance.

The next day, my focus and intent was so powerful that it was like a shot of adrenaline and I virtually went into a trance state as I styled the model's hair. I don't even remember what I did or how I did it, but the moment I saw the astonished look on my boss's face, I knew I had won my first competition. I continued to use this visualization technique to win competition after competition, and before each one, I gave thanks to God for providing success.

Later in life, when I met my yoga teacher, Swami Rama, I discovered that the process of visualization and manifestation is an ancient yoga science, thousands of years old. It is both eidetic and kinesthetic—you vividly *see* yourself doing something while also *feeling* yourself doing it. I applied this technique to many things, and eventually used it to build my products, my designs, my art, my businesses and my relationships. I also know many people who use it as a very effective healing technique that can even combat cancer.

The practice of meditation has helped me make the art of visualizing and manifesting very effective, by allowing me to slow down my mind and witness the whole process. It has also helped me to become better organized, and see the step-by-step stages of development. Meditation and prayer are both important tools for success, but often people misunderstand how they work.

Meditation is not concentration; it is not focusing on an idea in order to solve it, but bringing your mind to a state of silence. The highest state of consciousness is also the highest state of peace. Some people may use a candle flame or other images to visually focus on, others a *mantra* (sound syllables with positive meaning) to silently repeat in their mind, and others prefer to observe the flow of the breath. These are all simply devices to bring one to the sought-after state of blissful silent awareness and consciousness.

For the process of visualization, you could say meditation is like taking an eraser to clean the blackboard, so that afterwards, you will have a clean surface to clearly visualize whatever you want to manifest.

Meditation is Eastern in origin, whereas prayer is interpreted as being Western. Prayer, too, is often misunderstood. Prayer, for me, is gratitude. It is about surrendering to a higher power and thanking it for providing what you need. Ever since that starry night before my first hair styling competition, I have found giving thanks far more empowering than begging for grace.

Prayer and visualization also have far greater power if what we visualize or pray for is for the good of others rather than just for our self. Better yet, the prayer should be to create something for the good of future generations. When we ask God, the Divinity, or the Unnamed Intelligence of the Universe to make us an instrument to create something that will contribute to our planet's alivelihood, we will very likely succeed.

Positive Discipline

Once we develop our want-power and will-power, the next step is to develop our "can-power." We tell ourselves, "I *can* do it." After determining what we want and that we are committed to get it, we don't let any doubt enter our mind. With dynamic want-power, will-power, and can-power, we can accomplish any of our dreams—but only if we put together a plan of action. As Swami Rama used to say, "Life does not need to be changed; only our intents and actions do."

When we set up goals impulsively, we are likely to disappoint ourselves and weaken our will power. Why do New Year resolutions so often fail? Because we make a promise to ourselves but do not create a clear, concise plan of action; set up realistic commitments, agreements, and timelines; or get others involved in assisting, coaching and guiding us.

Once we determine the course of action, we can then apply "positive discipline" to help us stick to it. What is positive discipline? Many people apply *negative* discipline: they try *not* doing something (such as not overeating, not drinking alcohol, not taking drugs.) It is far more empowering to train ourselves to *do* something we have determined to do and follow through with it, no matter what. But I use the word *train* deliberately, because this kind of focus is not something we are in the habit of applying.

The ability to stay focused is a prime requirement for business and self-management, especially today, when we are bombarded with so many diversions and distractions. The ability to focus helps us to separate the part of our mind that is committed to achieving our goal from the part of our mind that wants to go on vacation or just hang out.

The skill of focusing a one-pointed mind requires daily practice. Our minds are constantly in a state of chatter and unrest. As soon as we determine to do one thing, our mind tries to talk us into doing another—it seems to simply be part of human nature. That's why the ancient yogis developed concentration techniques, as tools to focus the mind and achieve discipline. We can think about it in the same way we would think about building up our physical strength. If we want to build muscle, we take time out every day to exercise. We also pay attention to our diet, as our bodies need good nutrition to stay in shape. In the same way, to develop mental strength we must make it a daily practice, and set time aside for this purpose alone. We must also pay attention to our mental nutrition—replacing judgment and negativity with compassion and sympathy—because this is as important as physical nutrition.

We truly can achieve anything our minds can conceive; there are no limitations. But what separates the achievers from the non-achievers is that the former are committed to their goals and have developed the will-power and focus to see them through to completion.

There are no short cuts; self-discipline and perseverance is the only way. In the short term, perhaps we may feel discomfort, but the suffering will be much worse if we give in and then find ourselves unable to achieve our goals, because that lowers self-esteem and discourages us from further practice. In the long term, positive discipline brings only positive results.

Crisis = Opportunity

We all face many crises in our lives today—personal, professional and planetary. Often there are no quick, easy solutions, and at times the crisis may be so overwhelming that we cannot see a way through. But it is at times like these, I have discovered, that we are offered the greatest opportunities. When we encounter a crisis, we have come to a fork in the road where we have the opportunity to change direction and do something new rather than continue along the path that brought us to the crisis. Although we may not be able to see the new path, it is nevertheless there; it just may require a paradigm shift.

A paradigm shift is different than a change of mind. It is a shift from the mind to the heart; and that takes courage. The word courage is derived from the French word *coeur*, which means *heart*. And it takes great courage to break through our safe, familiar mindset and comfort zone and drop into our hearts and embrace a state of trust in the face of adverse circumstances.

I encountered the first great crisis of my life at the age of twenty. By that point, I had already earned a reputation as an internationally famous hairdresser and was invited to be a guest artist at the American Beauty Association's 1963 annual show in New York City. I was well received and soon after, I was invited back for a seminar tour. After two months, I had made more money than I would have earned in an entire year in Europe. It was my first taste of the American dream and I bought a Jaguar XKE convertible for cash.

One night, while on tour in Minneapolis, I took a fashion model out for dinner and got rear-ended on the highway by a drunk driver. My Jaguar was totaled, the model suffered a concussion, and I ended up in the hospital with several broken vertebrae. To make matters worse, neither I nor the other driver had auto insurance, and I had no health insurance. After two months in hospital, I was flat broke and owed a great deal of money in medical bills. The hospital confiscated my passport, leaving me with no choice but to stay in Minneapolis and take a job at a salon to pay off my debt.

So here I was: a young internationally acclaimed hair stylist at the top of my game, fresh from the most prestigious salons in Europe, suddenly injured, broke and stranded in a then-unfashionable city in the Midwest. I could have gotten very depressed if I had allowed myself to. Instead, I looked to see where there might be an opportunity, and I asked myself, "How can I best serve my customers?"

Within three months, I became the most sought-after hair stylist in the salon, with over four times the clientele of the other stylists. Soon after, with the help of a client who was head of a bank, I bought my first beauty salon, and within a year we had become the hottest new salon in town, and I had taken the first step on the road to many successful businesses—all because I saw a crisis as an opportunity.

We all have this capacity, because as a species, it is our biological nature. All living organisms create systems amongst themselves to sustain their own species in the face of crisis. If we observe the activity of a pine tree, for example, we can see that if the tree's life is endangered, it quickly produces pinecones, which carry the seeds of future trees. The pine tree's genetic code tells it to sustain the future of pine trees and it will do so until the moment of its death. It is fulfilling the purpose of all life—to continue and thrive.

Like a pine tree, we also carry this universal intelligence of sustainability. Human beings come equipped with two natural urges: to preserve the self, and to preserve everything to which the self is related. In our primitive state we are dominated by a personal survival instinct—"eat or be eaten"—but as we evolve, spiritually and culturally, it can evolve into a care for the survival of our species and the planetary system we are a part of.

When we encounter a personal or business crisis, therefore, the shift to opportunity is to shift the paradigm from, "How can I save my skin and serve myself?" to "How can I serve others and our planet?" If we follow sustainable principles and completely trust our inner power, wisdom and entrepreneurial spirit, the universe will support our efforts and reward us with success, for it will be the kind of success that the future of our planet is depending on.

Apprenticeship

Although I am sharing some of my life's experiences and lessons of success, I don't believe you can really learn someone else's philosophy by reading about it in a book; it has to be experienced directly—by discipleship or apprenticeship. Written or spoken philosophies are one-sided; they can't give us the feedback, discipline, or direct transmission we may need to learn and grow. Experience is the best source of knowledge, and if you can find someone whose abilities and wisdom you admire, become his or her apprentice. I was always an apprentice, and learned from many teachers.

My first apprenticeship was to my mother. She was an herbalist, and as a child, I went up into the mountains with her and helped carry down herbs and botanicals. When I became a successful hair stylist in America and opened my salon, she would visit every year, but she wasn't pleased with my chosen profession. She always complained of the smell of the chemicals. I disregarded her comments at first, but little did I realize how right she was. I would later learn that the main components in hairsprays and dyes were PVCs (polyvinyl chlorides) and other petrochemical-derived toxins, as well as synthetic chemical aromatics, all of which are harmful—especially in poorly ventilated salons.

One morning, I found myself unable to get out of bed; I was sick from all the chemicals and toxins, as well as exhausted from working long hours, partying and over-indulgence. Fortunately, my "healing crisis" occurred while my mother was visiting, and she quickly cured me with her herbs. From that point on, I became once again a student of my mother's herbalist arts. On her next visit, she brought herbs from the mountains of Austria, and we steamed them and then let them brew in the sun in brown bottles. We added essential oils and created our own product line, named *Horst,* also the name of my salon.

I discovered that I loved the art of mixing herbs and designing products, and I immersed myself in studies. An American Indian Medicine Man introduced me to jojoba oil, which he claimed was an amazing healing oil. I used it at the salon to massage clients' heads and bodies and to condition their hair, and also added it as an ingredient in my shampoos and conditioners—with astonishing results. Replacing synthetic chemicals with pure, aromatic botanicals made Horst products famous in the salons. My team and I were even called "The Jojoba's Witnesses"—affectionately by our customers and jokingly by our competitors. It was apropos, as we were evangelical about plants.

If you are ready to be an apprentice, many teachers will show up in your life. There is an ancient saying, "When the student is ready, the master appears." In 1967, I was a ripe and ready student and a great master appeared in my life—Dr. Swami Rama of the Himalayas.

Swami Rama was brought to the US to conduct

experiments in neuroscience by the Menninger Foundation, a world leader in psychiatric treatment, research and education. He had a medical degree from the University of Oxford, England, and claimed he could control his autonomic functions, for example, change his brain waves at will, stop his heartbeat, and change his body functions while in a deep sleep state. He also claimed he could communicate telepathically and perform other paranormal feats. I attended a lecture and witnessed one of these feats myself. It was also the first time I had heard someone speak about the mind/body relationship.

I realized then and there that I had found a very important teacher. I followed him to his ashram in Rishikesh, India, where he taught me yoga, meditation, and the art of Ayurveda—the ancient Indian science of healing with herbs and medicinal plants. I continued to study with him and with other medical doctors, plant scientists, ethno-botanists, anthropologists, shamans, and indigenous peoples around the world, while building up my business. Soon I was operating six salons and a cosmetology school, and in 1978 founded Aveda, derived from the Sanskrit word *A-veda*, which means *all nature's knowledge.*

Swami Rama later established a center in the United States where he trained medical doctors, clinical psychologists, nurses, other health care professionals, and students. His dream was to establish a medical city in the foothills of the Himalayas and he accomplished this by building a

250-acre, 1,000-bed hospital for the poor, an allopathic medical university, and a nursing school in Dehradun. Not only a great yogi, he was also an amazing entrepreneur who was totally selfless and gave everything to the local people. He left his physical body in 1996, and I had the honor, along with his son and two other devoted students, of dispersing his ashes in the Ganges river.

I have had many other teachers, and life itself is my apprenticeship. Some of my most important teachers have always been my customers. They are the other side of me. By paying attention to their needs, I have learned how to fulfill my own needs and the needs of our planet. And I consider nature to be my greatest teacher, and to her I always try to be a good, humble student.

Coming to our Senses

Our human body is indeed a model corporation. Our cells and organs work in perfect harmony twenty-four hours a day. They are active team members in the living organization, playing their parts as governed by their genetic programming and the information received through the senses. In nature, everything coexists and is designed to function until mental or physical dis-ease disrupts the system. It is our lack of understanding of our holistic coexistence that creates interferences with our biological functions and our relationships to the greater systems of which we are a part. If we study our body holistically, its systems and its functional design, we can learn to heal ourselves and others—and use it as a model for our relationships, our businesses, and our global systems.

The human body is made up of the same elements as our planet—soil, air, fire, and water. The element of soil forms the structure of our body—our bones and tissues. Air is our respiratory nutrition, and the fire of the sun gives us energy. Water is the matrix of life and makes up an amazing seventy-five percent of our body mass. We must always remember that the elements we are depleting, polluting and destroying in the world around us are the elements of our own bodies. Contributing to the destruction of our own elements is not sustainable. I believe that every human being carries the genetic codes to preserve and sustain the systems we are connected to, within and without. By becoming conscious of our holistic nature, we take the first step towards sustainable evolution for our planet.

Our senses are the gateway to understanding self and all that is interconnected. But these days our senses have become dulled by constant distraction, and we are acting and reacting in a primitive, unconscious way to the information they give us. Our brains are like intricate computers that get their information through our senses, in a process known as sensory perception. This data is stored and processed in our brain's operating system, which is called the limbic system. Everything we have ever smelled, tasted, seen, felt, or heard in our lives is stored in this very efficient data bank in our brains.

When we have a sensory experience, our brain goes on a search through its memory bank and informs us (consciously or subconsciously) as to whether we like or dislike the experience, or whether it was originally a nurturing experience or a painful one. This is a basic survival mechanism and we automatically have a response to these sense stimuli, which causes us to avoid pain or seek pleasure. It worked well in primitive times, but now life has become more complex, and the same system still operates by default. It's time to download a new operating system—for the way we conduct our transactions in our personal lives, in our companies, and with our planetary systems.

The ancient Yogis, Taoists, Buddhists, Christians,

Muslims/Sufis, American Indians, and all other indigenous cultures downloaded their information from nature itself. They instinctively knew what quantum physics is now discovering—that there is a vast ocean of information surrounding us, inside and out, that is similar to all the information on the internet. Information is vibrational frequency, which is part of our matrix of chemical matter. It flows through us and around us. Physicists call this "the quantum field," and author Deepak Chopra, M.D., refers to it as "the field of pure potentiality."

Scientists are just beginning to understand this information phenomenon, but have yet to discover the technology to access it. Enlightened physicists, however, like Fritjof Capra and Gary Zukov, are rediscovering how to apply ancient rituals to unravelling today's scientific mysteries and are coming up with fascinating revelations. The new theory of chaos physics, for example, informs us that events that were once considered random are linked to the rest of nature—a fact that the ancients knew thousands of years ago.

This is the matrix for a new personal and corporate operating system. We need to learn to connect, as the ancients did, to the information that surrounds us, and let that inform our thinking and our choices. From an early age, I've let myself be guided in this way. Perhaps because I am dyslexic and have never been one for reading too many books, I am convinced that much of what I know has come to me directly from the intelligence of nature itself. And I have discovered that while you can't *Google* it, you can access it through another portal: *prana,* which is Sanskrit for *breath of life*.

Our breath can be like a computer program that can actually help us plug into that sea of information. In every tradition that I have studied, from the Amazonian and African shamans to the American Indian medicine men to the yogis in the Himalayas, breath-regulation practices play a key role in daily life. These traditional medicine practitioners know, from wisdom passed down for thousands of years, that one of the best ways to become conscious of the Self is through awareness and control of the breath.

When we ground ourselves through the breath and move into a lower vibrational state, sometimes called the alpha state, we can attune ourselves to nature's information system, which is also the cosmic information system—the quantum field. Our thoughts are a cacophony of sensory accumulations that are in need of focus and direction. It is like being at a classical concert before it starts, where all the musicians are tuning their instruments at the same time. The sounds are awful because they're not in harmony, but when the conductor directs the musicians, the sound becomes beautiful and harmonious. Tuning ourselves in with our breath is like tuning our instruments in with the rest of the orchestra, giving us a feeling of joyful harmony, rather than discord, which we usually feel when our minds are vibrating at a higher, or beta wave frequency. The mind's information needs to be orchestrated and directed so that we can be in tune with our senses and the world they connect us to, and for this, we need to be our own conductors.

Through the practices of meditation, silence, contemplation and prayer, we can learn to quiet, focus and direct the mind, so that we can use it to access and manifest the infinite potentials and innate wisdom that is living all around us.

IN-VENTORY

How many of us do a daily inventory of our inner activities? Do we have a system in place to assess what has been traded mentally and emotionally each day and the effect it has had on our body and the people with whom we have interacted?

Every entrepreneur knows the importance of setting goals, then resetting and adjusting the actions taken to fulfill those goals on a daily basis. Similarly, each person's daily life requires the same degree of organization, planning and analysis. We should think of our lives as organizations and become more mindful of our transactions—of thoughts, words, feelings, emotions, and actions.

I started a practice of self-observation in 1968. It began when I started meditating and keeping a diary, and then it grew out of my life experiences and my exposure to various masters. Prior to that, I had never written anything down, or examined my emotions. Suddenly, I was writing every day and reading my notes from the day before. It was then that I began to see a cause-and-effect relationship between my actions and my emotions. Inspired, I started to analyze the cause-and-effect relationships in all the areas of my life, the way an entrepreneur analyzes all the facets of a business. This understanding of cause and effect is the central element of what I call the business of being, and it has also been the foundation of the model I used to build and manage my companies.

Imagine your life is a shop and you are the shopkeeper. At the end of the day, the smart shopkeeper conducts an inventory and considers how effective sales have been and adjusts plans in order to keep strategies that are working and change or eliminate those that are not. Likewise, professional athletes do an assessment of their performance after a game, and perhaps watch a slow-motion replay with their coaches to see what is working well and what they can improve. And movie directors watch each day's footage, to see if their vision is translating onto the screen, and to prepare for tomorrow in light of today's results. This is what we also need to do on a daily basis in our personal lives—an inventory, replay and self-coaching. Without a daily practice of self-observation, we are more prone to become stressed, insecure, and fearful, and therefore make decisions that we will later regret.

A daily program of mental cleansing through self-observation is the key to maintaining mental balance and rejuvenation, and if used regularly, it can enable us to direct the law of cause and effect and transform our lives.

Self-observation can be done any time and anywhere we can find a comfortable, private space in which to sit quietly and observe and slow down our chaotic, chattering mind. Once we have prepared ourselves through meditation, we are ready to conduct what I call an in-ventory, which is in essence a practice of contemplation.

In my in-ventory practice, I recall my day from the time

I woke up in the morning until the present moment. If the practice is done in the morning, I recall the actions of the previous day. Whenever an incident arises in which I had a personal or business transaction with someone, I try to observe it objectively, as if I were watching it in my own private screening room. And I don't watch it as a critic who evaluates what's right or wrong, but as a movie director sees if pain or bliss was created, and links the causes to the effects. As I watch my own "dailies," if I like what I see, I can move on to the next scene; if not, I can rewrite it, reenact it and reshoot it. After all, it's my movie and I am the director.

If we want to improve our performance, all we need to remember is to be true to our true selves, and to life's purpose or mission. Of course, this is not an easy task, as we have lost our "original face," as the Zen masters call it, and have identified with a false sense of self. One of the ways we can reclaim our true self is with the in-ventory process. As we regulate and balance our breathing, it will provide the calmness and peace that is the source of self. In that space, we can re-create our life's purpose or mission and set goals. Then, regardless of all of the habits and conditioning that usually hinder us, we can focus on our goals and mission statement and let them guide us to take the correct action steps. The best time to plan action steps is right after the in-ventory process when the mind is still fresh and calm.

The daily in-ventory is how I have generated all of my successes in life as well as maintaining a state of internal balance. Whenever I encounter a crisis, upset, or stressful situation, I withdraw and access that blissful silent state, which is readily available to each of us, where I can see myself in the clear reflection of a focused mind. I also practice self-observation with others, as this brings an even greater degree of objectivity to the process. When we have learned to do an in-ventory on ourselves, we can then learn to do it in our families, our relationships and our businesses.

PART II:

WE, INC. - THE HOLISTIC CORPORATION

"This, in a nutshell, is the challenge . . . to create social and cultural environments in which we can satisfy our needs without diminishing the opportunities and options of future generations to satisfy their needs. And this is also the challenge of ecologically conscious management: to modify corporate growth by introducing sustainability as a key criterion for all business activities."

- Fritjof Capra

Living Systems

Becoming an Eco-preneur

I believe one of the best ways to start a new sustainable business is to first change our lifestyle; then let our new lifestyle become our business. When we start eating organic foods, for example, we will become aware of how the organic business is booming. Organic farming has doubled over recent years and is one of the most profitable sectors in agriculture today—a perfect opportunity for eco-preneurs who want to serve the planet and its people and be successful at the same time.

Another way to change course is to look at our current situation and ask, "How can I serve my customers better?" It's never ceased to amaze me how much can be revealed through asking this simple question. Recently, I gave a lecture at the Learning Annex on "How to Start a Sustainable Business." For the first half of the lecture, I did not talk about the steps to starting a business, which many people had been expecting; I spoke instead about "the business of being"—explaining the importance of understanding our interconnectedness and interdependency with all of life. About half way through the lecture, a woman from the audience asked, "What does all this have to do with starting a sustainable business?"

I could feel her frustration; she had come to learn the steps, but she was failing to comprehend that I had just presented her with the first and most important one. So

I asked her what her career path was. She said she was a nurse and was frustrated with the unsustainable hospital system and wanted to leave her job and start a new career.

I said: "You don't need to go anywhere. Crisis equals opportunity! If you want to make a difference, first ask yourself: 'How can I serve my customers—my patients—better? What's needed in the nursing profession to make it sustainable?' You could make healthy products for nurses, from essential oils and aromatics, such as natural, organic moisturizers or ointments for massage and to heal bedsores. Provide visualization tapes to help patients feel better and participate in their own healing process. Provide holistic midwifery. Then you could create a school or training course to educate other nurses in a new model of holistic, sustainable nursing."

I was also a nurse, in a sense; that's part of what a hair stylist is. Clients brought their problems and wounds to be healed when they sat in my chair; they didn't just bring their hair. So I listened and served them and made them feel beautiful while I made them look beautiful.

Then I learned about business from my clients and their husbands, who were accountants, lawyers and successful businesspeople. I allowed them to serve me, and some of my clients were instrumental in helping me start up my businesses.

That is a great gift you can give others—to allow them to serve you. When we give to others, inadvertently we make them beholden to us. But when we allow them to help us, we empower them by bringing out their gift to serve, and then we create a beautiful dynamic by serving each other, and that is the foundation for sustainable success.

Corporate Lessons from the Rainforest

If we want our business to be environmentally friendly and sustainable, we need to connect to the people and places we are trying to protect—both emotionally and intellectually. Too many people who are championing "green" values—both businessmen and activists—are shockingly uninformed about the issues they are standing for, and have often never directly seen or experienced the devastation that irresponsible business practice creates.

We in the corporate world would do well to spend time amongst our indigenous peoples. Because we are a technologically advanced society, we think of ourselves as being very sophisticated. The word *sophisticated,* however, in its primary definition in the Merriam-Webster dictionary is: "not in a natural state, deprived of nature or original simplicity; highly complicated or developed." This is all too true of most of us, and while the indigenous peoples may lack our "sophistication," they more than make up for it in earth wisdom, which has traditionally been passed down through thousands of years. Unfortunately, we are in danger of losing that wisdom, as we are destroying the rainforests, jungles and wilderness that nurture their cultures, along with valuable healing plant species.

In 1992, I was invited by the United Nations Global Forum to speak at the Earth Summit in Rio de Janeiro,

Brazil—a global gathering to address the earth crisis, which included religious leaders, business leaders, indigenous chieftains, scientists, politicians, artists, members of the Brazilian parliament, and international press. It was here that I met, for the second time, the then-Senator Al Gore, who delivered the keynote address. I was tremendously motivated by his clear understanding of the condition of our planet and his vision of what needed to be done economically and ecologically to restore it—and in so doing, create a whole new business opportunity!

The last speaker of the conference was a shaman from the Brazilian Amazon. His tribe lived deep within the rainforest, over two weeks' journey from the nearest town. Although he was small and thin, he appeared strong in structure, uniquely energetic and had a special radiance about him. He was covered in body paint and wore a feathered headdress. He approached the podium and apologized for the fact that what he was about to say were not his ideas or words but those of the spirits of the rainforest who were speaking through him.

His Holiness the Dalai Lama, who was sitting in front of me, leaned forward with anticipation, and the entire room became hushed and attentive to what this small, unassuming shaman was about to say. The shaman calmly declared that all the previous speakers did not really know what they were talking about, because they, like all other people in the modern civilized world, were desensitized and not in daily communication with the spirit of the earth and the spirit of nature. As he spoke, a chill ran up and down my spine. I felt that he was indeed channeling the spirits, and I knew that I had to journey into the rainforest and meet his tribe. My business instincts joined forces with my spiritual instincts when I later attended the Indigenous Conference and saw the beautiful colors of the body paint the tribal people wore—colors that would be perfect for the cosmetic line I was creating.

On my first trip to the Amazon, I saw firsthand the effects of the destruction of the environment on the plant and animal species and the indigenous peoples. I also learned some of the most important business lessons of my life. I found it quite a revelation to experience the wisdom and intelligence of the tribe and live among them in the rainforest.

My business systems have always been built around teams, and I learned a lot about team management from the tribal people. Their systems were very impressive, with each person's role clearly defined. All members of the tribe participated in choosing their leaders. Every member of the tribe shared the raising, education, and protection of the children, which included teaching them the skills of safety and sustainability. I never experienced competition and conflict amongst the men, women, and children during my entire stay with them—even in their games. Nor did I encounter any depressed or angry people.

I also learned from them about living, working and worshipping in harmony with nature's rhythms. Their religious practice was the worship of plants and the cycles of nature. Cleansing their body was part of their daily morning worship, as was painting each other's bodies with plant, mineral, and animal materials. All the body paints had medicinal value and provided protection from insects and sun exposure. They had no dumping grounds and nothing was thrown away; everything was composted, recycled, repaired, or shared. Food was distributed equally and shared with the animals, and eating was also part of their worship.

Another great lesson I learned was from the process by which they interviewed me before agreeing to work with Aveda to produce colors for our cosmetic line. The tribe had requested that I bring a family member with me, and not only was I asked to speak about myself and my mission, but my daughter, who I had chosen to accompany me, was asked to speak and give her evaluation of me as a person, a father, and a businessman. The process of interviewing and deliberations took three days, and at the end of that period the tribal leaders agreed to work with us and we drew up an agreement, becoming the first foreign company to set the precedence for intellectual property rights to do business with indigenous peoples in Brazil. Their method of decision-making made a lasting impression on me, and to this day, when I am interviewing someone for an important position,

I try to create social situations in which I can meet a partner or family member, as this is one of the best ways to assess the potential sustainability of a business relationship.

We used a deforested area to plant and the tribe members built ingenious greenhouses out of shrubs and leaves. Then they gathered and transplanted about 250,000 seedlings. In turn, we helped the tribe, as they did not need to sell their land to logging or mining companies for income, and there was no clear-cutting, which destroys many plant and animal species. We provided them with medical care and helped them create financial sustainability, while leaving them free to live according to their own tradition, preserving their language and culture. The first product we created together was a lipstick with the herbal color *uruku,* which is used today in many of Aveda's products.

It is one of my greatest wishes that the corporate world will learn to respect, appreciate, and support the indigenous peoples, for they are our greatest allies and representatives to the natural world. What we fail to realize is that if we lose our indigenous peoples, we are losing an important part of ourselves. They are the members of our species who live at the point of impact in our biosphere, and if we listen to them, they can tell us when things are going wrong. Just as the animals were able to sense the recent tsunami wave long before any of our instruments could, indigenous peoples also have fine-tuned sensitivity to the natural world. They know many things long before our guys in white coats because they are still in tune with nature. That's why I listen to them; they are my greatest consultants. Working with the Amazon tribe on the color project for Aveda was one of the most rewarding experiences in all my years with the company.

I encourage anyone who either leads or works for a corporation, or even anyone who buys consumer products, as we all do, to spend time on the front lines—to visit the places where their products are made and the people who make them. I have always traveled the world in search of sources and ingredients for my products, and my passion for making a difference has grown out of meeting not only the businesspeople but the farmers, the field-workers, and their families. It has been fueled by seeing for myself the devastation caused by irresponsible business practices, and empowered by discovering how I could serve and support the indigenous peoples and the planet.

We all need to educate ourselves to *feel* these things, because it is only through feeling that we will find the real vision and mission, the motivation and passion to make a difference. We should make ourselves the apprentices of those who serve our businesses and make our products, so that we may discover how we can serve them and how together we can serve our shared environment.

BIODYNAMIC BUSINESS

The holistic movement has been mainly associated with body/mind medicine. It is a model that is concerned with the whole system rather than with the analysis and treatment of parts. Holistic ecology, which we now call sustainability, views mankind and the environment as a single, whole system. Although I have practiced the holistic approach in the salon, spa, product manufacture and retail business for thirty-five years, it is still relatively new to business management.

As a student of nature and its laws, one model that I like to use is that of "biodynamic business." Biodynamic agriculture is the oldest organic approach to farming and gardening, and the most sustainable. Its principles are founded on a biological, holistic, and spiritual understanding of nature that goes back to the beginning of agriculture, where farmers simply learned to use nature's laws in growing food. It was reintroduced in the early twentieth century by Rudolf Steiner, the great Austrian schoolteacher, philosopher, scientist, and social reformer.

Biodynamics is a methodology that goes above and beyond organic. Before planting seeds, the soil must be detoxified of insecticides and pesticides for three years, allowing it to purify and rejuvenate. Then, prior to fertilization, a special compost mixture of six medicinal plants—yarrow, chamomile, stinging nettle, oak, dandelion and valerian—is added to enrich the soil to its maximum potential. The fertilizer is then composed of manure from animals that live on the land and have been biodynamically fed. Next, the planting is done in accordance with the lunar cycle, as the moon has a dynamic effect on the earth's atmospheric condition and influences the growth cycles of the soil.

These same principles, I have found, can be applied to a business context. The "seed" is the *intent* of the business. It's the idea and the desire, and when it's cultivated and nurtured, it sprouts, grows, and multiplies.

The "soil" is the business environment, and must be detoxified. We can start with physical detoxification by eliminating toxic substances from our office and providing clean air, lots of plants, filtered water and encouraging employees to adopt a healthy, mostly organic diet.

Then we can turn our attention to emotional and spiritual detoxification—the elimination of fear and pain by identifying its causes through daily in-ventory, and the transformation of our illusion of a separate self—our "independency"—into an "inter-dependency."

Once we have detoxified the soil, we can add a special compost of ethics, values, and sustainability, which include: a commitment to superlative customer service; team ownership; product purity; socially and environmentally responsible practices; fair trade; non-violence; non-exploitative labor; reduction and elimination of waste;

ongoing education of team members; motivation and reward systems; and charity and philanthropy

Finally, in order to consider ourselves biodynamic, we should try to cultivate our business according to natural cycles. We don't have to build it around lunar cycles, but we can support the natural ebb and flow of the energy of our team.

After formulating a line of sustainable, plant-based products, I wanted to create a sustainable, socially responsible environment for my employees and have them participate in building the organization. I considered the surroundings they worked in to be very important because they were going to spend a great deal of time there. My initiative in all my business ventures has been support the teams' physical and mental environments by providing things like organic cafeterias, yoga classes, massage sessions, day care centers, gyms, bikes and hiking trails for nature breaks, and silent rooms for contemplation and stress relief. I even installed a pool table where we could relax or shoot pool while brainstorming. Why sit in a room with four walls and no windows when you're trying to expand your creativity? A think tank doesn't have to be in a tank!

We subsidized our organic cafeteria so the employees could afford it, as I didn't want them to work on developing natural, organic products and then go to the local fast food chains for lunch. However, it was hard to convince our factory workers because many of them still had super-size habits, so we had to educate them. Once a week, we conducted a seminar for the entire staff, bringing in speakers to lecture on such meaningful subjects as biodiversity, preventable causes of cancer, and the benefits of organic agriculture and products.

Just as biodynamic agriculture in a single farm works in harmony with the cycles that support the entire planet, the holistic mission of a biodynamic business should reach beyond its products and corporate environment. At Aveda, our mission was also about respecting all cultures. We created products for people of all different races and ethnic backgrounds. We created hair care products for curly hair, straight hair, highly textured hair, and smooth hair, and natural cosmetics to help people from all cultures balance their skin tone. We became globally successful because we recognized that true, natural beauty is a universal ideal.

Our goal was also to promote sustainability for the planet and its peoples through everything we used to create our products. We sourced plant-derived raw materials from fifty-four different countries all over the world, working directly with the indigenous peoples and supporting their communities as they supplied our business. Today, I invest in local farms and plantations for raw materials for my Intelligent Nutrients products. I want to be sure that I am getting exactly what I pay for when I order organic ingredients that are free of chemical additives, not tested on animals, and do not exploit farm workers. The only way I can be certain of this is to go directly to the source—a practice I call "pure sourcing." It's much more time-consuming and expensive to create a product this way, but when it comes to sustainability, you can't cut corners on integrity.

The causes of all dis-ease—physical, mental, and environmental—are linked to our psychological and physiological environments, and the interpersonal environments of our relationships. By following biodynamic business principles and creating holistic companies, we can make business the healer of our bodies and our ecosystem, rather than a carrier of dis-ease.

TEAM-SYSTEMS

Human beings are always forming teams and partnerships—in our personal lives and in our businesses. But often, in our relationships and partnerships, we're not really working together. Unless there is a truly shared vision, the parties remain self-centered, and then the "we" just becomes a bigger "me." This gives rise to the systems and structures we see in place throughout the corporate world today—systems of top-to-bottom management, which I feel create a huge moral and work ethic problem.

Top-to-bottom management does not work holistically to benefit all. Fear, greed, and anger motivates everyone to seek the top layers, where there is more pay, more social status, more security, and more opportunities to enrich the self. This kind of management breeds caste systems, which we see throughout our society.

Nature does not operate like we humans do; it is not as competitive. Nature's system is holistic—it nurtures the entire system and does not isolate any individual part. Physicist and author Fritjof Capra, a fellow Austrian born fifteen minutes from my hometown, has studied living systems extensively, and he explains that in any living community or organization, the law of natural success applies: the success of the organization is dependent upon the contribution of its members, while the success of the member is dependent upon the system as a whole.

We need to follow and study the laws of nature if we ever are going to make a difference on this planet, surrender our egos and join the healing paradigm. The healing begins when we unite around a vision that takes into account the wellbeing of the system as a whole. Then we create a beautiful dynamic by serving each other, and that is the foundation for great teamwork and a holistic business management system.

My management style was self-taught. Because of my lack of education, I never believed that I was smart enough to make a lone decision. During my salon years, I started "storyboarding" all our business activities and projects on my days off. Every team member at the salons participated in building the story, and after the story was built the team members were asked to volunteer which part of the story they would commit to manifest and accomplish before the next weekly meeting. I used the same methods when I started the cosmetic company—when major decisions had to be made the team voted and the majority ruled.

As the cosmetic company grew, we had more teams, and they got bigger, until the process got slower and it was more difficult to function. As a result, team leaders were voted for by team members. Team leaders did not make decisions—their job was to manage the agenda, time, and objectives and make sure that everybody, including themselves, was participating in the decision-making process. Human Resources provided ongoing training to old and new employees. I jokingly called HR "the medicine society," as they had to make sure all employees were in balance and keep the members of the team-systems aligned.

Sometimes, when we had to hire people from outside, who were used to working in top-to-bottom systems, they would complain that there were too many meetings. What they didn't understand was that in these meetings people were making decisions and commitments, to which they were held accountable. In our holistic company, every day of work was synergistic due to these meetings. We shared decisions, goals, celebrations, team and individual achievements, and new challenges. When we met, we would sit in front of a big screen, so that we weren't looking at each other, but at the goals, commitments, and steps we were creating together. Ours was a paradigm of team ownership, in which profits are shared on a team performance basis, not on an individual basis.

I have always believed every member of the company has a right to ownership, which is earned by contribution to the growth and preservation of the company. I may have founded different businesses, but it was always the team that made them successful—the dedication, commitment, and selfless service of all.

Learning to Listen

There is a tremendous amount of energy and money lost in business because of poor communication. The key to communication is listening, and if we want our businesses to be sustainable and successful, we all need to learn to listen better.

I know from experience that when I speak to individuals or groups, the vast majority are not listening to what I'm saying. Why? They are too busy listening to their own interpretation of what I am speaking about. As we listen to someone speak, we are filtering what we hear through our own sensory memories and associations with painful, fear-based, or pleasurable experiences.

Once we understand and become aware of our sensory mechanism, we will have a greater ability to respond appropriately to the present moment and not get affected by reactions based on past experiences. If we practice observing the emotional reactions and feelings in our body that cause constriction or pain, and then learn to release them through our breath, we can center ourselves in the present moment and respond with a true sense of personal power. We can then also empower the other person by being fully attentive to their needs.

Real communication, as I understand it, needs to be done in person. Memos, and their modern incarnation, emails, are a poor means of communication, because they are not an effective way to find out what people's needs are. If I need to get a decision or commitment to get something accomplished, it has to be live—by phone or in person. Perhaps it's not easy to find people for a dialogue but it's still the best way to get a solid commitment, with total clarity. Emails and memos are okay for less important dialogue, but when it comes to a fully agreed upon commitment, they will never replace a handshake, a hug or a look in the eye.

Human beings are constantly interpreting, and a great deal of team management or any business relationship comes down to the art of keeping everyone on the same page. Any hair stylist who has given a client a "short" cut as requested, only to be met with a horrified "not that short!" knows that language is a clumsy and relative tool. Whenever I enter into a commitment, I tell the other parties my interpretation of the commitment, and we all agree on that before writing it down on paper and signing it as a legally binding document. I always tell myself, my friends and my colleagues, "never finish a dialogue without reinterpretation and commitment."

Cloning Ourselves

In the not-too-distant future it may be possible to clone ourselves. When it comes to a human body, I would say one of us is probably enough. But if we want to clone our passion for life, our skills, or our desire to make a difference on this planet, we already have that ability—and in fact, it is one of our greatest assets if we want to create a sustainable business.

In the early days of my salon business, we grew very quickly, and became inundated with new clients. I needed good stylists to work for me. Unfortunately, those I hired were not well trained and it took hard work and long hours to improve them. And then as soon as they had learned my techniques and developed a following, they would leave for better paid positions or open their own salons and compete against me! That left me with the task of hiring new stylists and starting the training process all over again. It was a tremendous source of frustration and stress—until I turned the crisis into another opportunity.

I shifted the paradigm of how I was viewing the whole situation, and began to understand that my problem was the very nature of the salon business: stylists wanted to learn from me because I was famous and successful, but they were also entrepreneurs, just as I had been. So instead of resenting their attitude, I asked myself, "What could I do to serve them?"

As soon as I looked at it from this perspective, the opportunity was obvious: open a training center for hair stylists. Or even better, open a school for cosmetology: massage, skin care, spa care and hair care. In 1970, I founded the Horst Institute. Now aspiring hair stylists would pay to learn my techniques, and those who excelled, I would hire. I wasn't even concerned as to whether or not the Institute itself would be successful; I was using it to train potential employees in a way that didn't cost me money or waste my time and energy.

As it turned out, the Horst Institute became one of the most successful cosmetology schools in the country. The key to its success, however, was not my skills or business ability, but my vision—I envisioned it as a holistic training center rather than just a beauty school. It was a synergetic combination of service, product, sales, and education and it immediately changed the whole dynamics of the business. I believe that all of today's businesses need a customized internal education system designed to function for the specific needs of the company.

INTELLIGENT INNOVATION

Fortunately, future-minded CEOs and executives are waking up to the fact that a healthy planet is good for the bottom line and a healthy office environment is good for employees. Unfortunately, there's still a lot of waking up to do about the fact that a holistic, sustainable company must revolve around a holistic, sustainable product. Ethical and socially responsible business practices are a great start, but if the product does not meet holistic, sustainable standards, then, as far as I am concerned, it's not truly ethical nor socially responsible.

It takes eco-preneurs to recognize the opportunity in the current global crisis, and create innovative products and services that are truly sustainable. Ecopreneurialism is the promise of success for the future, because it is focused on providing people with systems and products that nurture and sustain their bodies, spirits, and environment.

I had founded a highly successful cosmetic company, and built it around holistic and sustainable principles and products, in a way that was revolutionary for the industry at the time. But ultimately the lesson I learned was that the term "cosmetic" itself is outdated. That which is cosmetic is by nature artificial and superficial. Today, I am trying to go beyond cosmetic and nurture our outer beauty from within. As I became interested in nutrition, I came to the conclusion that everything we put on our bodies or in our working and living environment should be nutritional—nurturing us on every level of our being. It was this growing understanding that inspired me to reinvent myself and found Intelligent Nutrients, as a means of finding greater completion in my life's mission and continuing my service to my customers—the planet and all its people.

Offering real alternatives, products and services which help the planet and its people to function, is today's and the future's business opportunity. We only have to look at the crises in our world to begin to see the opportunities they hold. For example, the water business is booming. We are running out of pure water as a result of pollution, overpopulation, wastage, and global climate change. These days we are fighting oil wars, but future wars may be fought over water. So if we can think of new, innovative ways to conserve and purify water, it can provide an invaluable service and lead to sustainable success.

The business of sun protection and solar power presents another huge opportunity. The sun is destroying organic life because of ozone depletion and skin cancer has increased by seventy-five percent since 1965, according to the Cancer Prevention Coalition. These are realities we cannot escape, but we can manage them, by changing our lifestyle, and through paying attention to our own needs, letting our new lifestyle become our business. The potentials for new products are here in all the elements that make up both our bodies and our world. When we come up with creative ideas for purifying air, soil, and water; for harnessing the energy of the sun; and for making products that eliminate harmful emissions and waste; then we are in business—sustainable business.

Almost everything that is produced, designed and manufactured today is somehow related to petrochemicals. And not only are the petrochemical industries the biggest polluters of our planet, they are also depleting the earth of its natural lubrication. Biodynamically, crude oil is related to plant root resinoids through the mineral system, and forms underground resinoid rivers and lakes. They are very old and play an important role in the earth's biological systems. The products we create from petrochemicals, such as much of the packaging on consumer goods, come from a "natural" source but are certainly not biodegradable, which means they will never return to the earth from which they came. Before we cause irreversible damage to our planet, we need to make the transition from a petrochemical society to a carbohydrate society—one in which we create products and packaging out of biodegradable materials that can be recycled by the earth. We already have the capacity to do this—we just need to wake up to the urgency. Then we could begin to use plants—our natural life support system, which already purify our air, shelter our bodies, and provide us with medicine and food—as the building blocks of our consumer goods also.

My friend and one of my most important teachers, Dr. Michael Braungart, a brilliant chemist and co-author with architect William McDonough of *Cradle to Cradle,* is one of the leading visionaries in this field. He looks at sustainability as the next evolution of industrialism. He says there is a new breed of young scientists who are pursuing what he calls "evolutionary design." Their products are built according to a "cradle to cradle" paradigm: there is no waste, because everything becomes a nutrient—either a technical nutrient that is reusable in future products and services, or a biological nutrient. For example, he envisions a car as a "nutra-vehicle," which can collect nitrogen from its exhaust and turn it into fertilizer. All its emissions are consumable and ultimately the car itself can be consumed in the new production line.

This was also the vision of the great scientist/inventor R. Buckminster Fuller, almost half a century ago. He was truly a man ahead of his time. His lifelong goal was the development of what he called "Comprehensive Anticipatory Design Science"—an attempt to anticipate and solve humanity's major problems through the highest technology by providing "more and more life support for everybody, with less and less resources." Bucky Fuller, as we affectionately called him, was one of the earliest proponents of renewable energy sources, which he incorporated into his designs. He claimed, "There is no energy crisis, only a crisis of ignorance." His research demonstrated that humanity could satisfy 100% of its energy needs while phasing out fossil fuels and atomic energy. Bucky Fuller was way ahead of the curve, and I hope, for our planet's sake, that the curve is finally catching up with him.

Today, we are "the curve." If we want to rise to the peak of our potentiality and purpose in this life, let us become part of the sustainable evolution and look to see what contribution we can make to the planet, while contributing to our own success. There are many great opportunities just on the horizon, and we will begin to see them when we learn to tune in to the needs of our planet.

If we listen to the call of the present, we will find out what is needed for the future. I try to stay attuned to changes in our planet, not just through what I read in the news or the science or medical journals, but through listening to indigenous people; who know because they listen to the earth. To paraphrase John F. Kennedy, "Ask not what your planet can do for you; ask what you can do for your planet." I always thought Kennedy's speechwriter must have been a biologist, because his original words could only have been written by someone who understood the laws of living systems. Funnily enough, when I said that in a lecture a few years ago, a woman in the audience stood up and said, "You're right. It was my father, and he was a biologist."

So if we are not working for companies that think like biologists, or at least are willing to start doing so, we should change companies or start our own. It's time to get the eco-preneurial spirit, and make our work a worship—a means of giving thanks and giving something back to the earth that gave us life. Let's not just make a living—let's make alivelihood for our planet.

PART III:

EARTH, INC. - THE ART OF SUSTAINABLE SUCCESS

"Rather than lamenting the human ecological footprint, [we can] conceive systems in which the flow of materials in the human economy supports the Earth's life systems while providing more people with more of what they need and love.
Enduring wealth replaces endless waste; stories of hope outshine the tragic strategies of the past.
Why not leave a footprint worth celebrating?"

– Michael Braungart & William McDonough
Re-Inventing the World

Enlightened Capitalism

Creating a sustainable corporate operating system is just the first step. This new paradigm has to then become a force for changing the global system itself. We're in a planetary crisis/opportunity and it's going to take more than just changing one corporation at a time to shift the global economic model rooted in greed, fear, self-interest, and exploitation.

I recently had the opportunity to listen to former Vice President Al Gore lecture once again, this time at the Science Museum in Minneapolis. In front of a packed auditorium, he presented the latest scientific evidence on climate change from around the world. I wish he could have been heard by all the people in the media, government, and business who doubt and criticize the environmental community for its stance on climate change, and feel that the solutions proposed are simply not economically feasible. These people exemplify Bucky Fuller's "crisis of ignorance." Gore's message was simple: that the next evolution of our global economy *is* solving the global crisis. How could they be separate? If our natural systems collapse, a strong economy will be useless. But if we have courage and faith in the scientific evidence that is readily available, and stop denying the reality that confronts us, we can build a new global economy that will in itself be the solution. My personal feeling is that we need leaders like Al Gore to guide us in this endeavor—and more than anything, we need eco-preneurs to come together and fuel it with innovation and passion.

We need to act collectively to cause a critical mass, by forming alliances with like-minded eco-preneurs and organizations. We need to make sustainability the new bottom line, in our lifestyles, in our culture, and in our business ventures. As Fritjof Capra puts it: "This, in a nutshell, is the challenge . . . to create social and cultural environments in which we can satisfy our needs without diminishing the opportunities and options of future generations to satisfy their needs. And this is also the challenge of ecologically conscious management: to modify corporate growth by introducing sustainability as a key criterion for all business activities."

Shifting the milieu of the corporate world will take qualities not often found in today's boardrooms: patience and perseverance. Corporations are always looking for shortcuts in the race for profit. If a company doesn't make a profit in two years, the CEO or President is gone. Business is focused on short-term gain rather than long-term sustainability. Instead of looking at being of service, management is looking at the bottom line just so they can stay on top. Publicly traded companies cannot see beyond satisfying their shareholders—and the very laws that bind them keep this mindset in place. Corporations have a legal mandate to protect their shareholders' investments—even at the expense of their employees, suppliers, customers and the environment. In fact, there is a term for all these factors in the corporate language: "externalities." These are figured into the cost-benefit equations businesses use to make decisions, and the only criteria is the benefit to the bottom line.

I consider this the dinosaur approach to business. The law of anthropology states that the species who survive are not the biggest and strongest but the most adaptable. And how do we adapt? I say, by becoming more sustainable. The industrial revolution is the dinosaur; the future is the sustainable evolution. Our companies operate like machines, driven by numbers and built on mechanistic principles. As Peter Senge, author of the classic *The Fifth Discipline* said in a recent interview for *What Is Enlightenment?* magazine, "You can't approach a business as if it were a machine and expect it not to operate in blind, machine-like ways vis-à-vis the larger communities and living systems of which it is a part." We need to change the way we think about not only our own business systems, but the larger corporate systems in which they are embedded. We need to educate ourselves and our shareholders in sustainable principles, and ultimately we need to rewrite the laws of business to reflect our responsibilities not only to our human shareholders but to our greater shareholder, which is nature itself.

If you're in corporate management and want to increase your bottom line without eroding it, sustainability is the way to do it. If you need convincing, or if your shareholders need convincing, read *The Natural Step for Business* by Brian Nattras & Mary Altomare, or *Natural Capitalism* by Paul Hawken.

The Natural Step cites Ray Anderson, CEO of Interface Corporation, a $1.4 billion company that developed the first recyclable floor coverings and solar-powered manufacturing plant. In the first four years of its sustainable QUEST program, his company saved approximately $75 million.

"Sustainability is the key word for the future," states Anders Moberg, President of the enormously successful IKEA Corporation. Unlike environmentalism, which corporations view as a threat to their bottom line, sustainability creates opportunities to gain competitive advantage, reduce costs, enhance profits, increase employee loyalty and morale, reduce staff turnover, stimulate new product innovation, and increase market share while improving the health of both planet and people.

In addition to IKEA, more than sixty corporations in Sweden have implemented the Natural Step sustainability program, including Electrolux, Swedish Railways, Scandia (Sweden's largest hotel chain), and even McDonald's. In the US, corporations such as Home Depot, Nike, and Mitsubishi USA have also adopted the Natural Step program. And organizations like Social Venture Network and Businesses for Social Responsibility, where many small and large companies have joined to promote sustainable principles, are making great contributions.

We are entering a new economic era, according to Lester Brown, author of *Eco-Economy: Building an Economy for the Earth* and head of the World Watch Institute in Washington, D.C. He asserts that this new "eco-economy" will far surpass the industrial revolution in new business opportunities: "No sector of the global economy will be untouched. . . . Those who anticipate the emerging eco-economy and plan for it will be the winners. Those who cling to the past risk becoming part of it."

On this emerging new playing field, small players with big visions will have the capacity make a big impact—not just in rebelling against the established corporate paradigm, but in working to shift the paradigm itself. Even the big players, the corporate giants, can be redirected—and indeed, if things are really going to change it is essential that they are. How do we affect a giant corporation? That was my intent when I sold Aveda to Estée Lauder. Many people warned me: "Don't sell out to the cosmetic giant. They will destroy your mission." But I felt just the opposite. I felt that the sustainable and socially responsible business practices and products that Aveda supported could help to turn the direction of Estée Lauder. And if Estée Lauder could change its direction, it would in turn affect corporate America, and ultimately help to transform the world. That's what I call "enlightened capitalism." It's not about blaming capitalism for the crisis, but seeing the creative force of human entrepreneurialism as the ultimate solution.

So we should never think we can't make a difference; in the interconnected web of life, everything matters. Our every action sends ripples across the universe. As individuals we can make a difference, but as individuals sticking together, we can make an impact. Snowflakes are the most delicate, fragile forms of matter in nature, but look at what happens when a lot of them stick together. Have you ever seen an avalanche? Let's become a creative avalanche that can reshape the landscape of our future. We need to make sustainability fashionable, honorable, heroic, and chic. Ultimately, we need to add it to our religions and our belief systems, because after all, it is about worshipping God in all that we are interconnected with. We humans do not have a choice "to be or not to be," so let us all invest in our future.

Consumer Democracy

We are living in confusing times. The companies who are contributing to the depletion of our earth's life-support systems are also creating foundations to help fight and cure diseases. Their leaders are often unaware that the products they manufacture and sell may be the cause of the diseases their foundations are set up to help cure. The sad truth is that there is a growing marketing trend known as "greenwashing" which simply aims to make a corporation look like it is doing something good for the planet and its people. Who's to blame? The corporations? We've become them; the corporate body is made up of us, our friends, the people we know and went to school with. The politicians? We've voted them into office. It's time to wake up, stop blaming, and realize that we each have the power to be the solution—because we live in a consumer democracy.

We are all consumers and we are all producers in one form or another. It has always been explained to me that one of the foundations of a true, democratic society is "the right to know." Unfortunately, as consumers, we are deprived of this right. Manufacturers and marketers of consumer products do not tell the truth about what their products contain and what impacts they have on the human body and our environmental body. And the sad fact is that the vast majority of consumers simply don't know, don't want to know, or don't know how to know.

Those of us who care about ourselves and our planet need to take action. In our consumer democracy, we may not be getting the knowledge that is our right, but we can cast our vote. How do we vote? We vote with what we buy. We consumers have a responsibility to ourselves and our planet and can no longer afford to be passive and naïve. We must educate ourselves to make responsible choices in what we buy and how we live. We must remind ourselves every day that we vote with what we buy.

It's difficult to know what we are voting for when we make a purchase. Consumers are kept ignorant about harmful ingredients in household and cosmetic products. These products list chemical names which even chemists have difficulty pronouncing or identifying. While some labels warn us: "Do not ingest," or "Keep away from children," many of the most harmful and cancer-causing ingredients do not have to be ingested to be absorbed. Our bodies assimilate medicinal, nutritional, and toxic chemicals in many ways—through inhalation, skin absorption, and other orifices. Having worked with chemists on cosmetic products for more than thirty years, I can verify that toxic chemicals can enter our bodies without us needing to swallow them.

Samuel Epstein, M.D., Professor Emeritus Environmental & Occupational Medicine at the University of Illinois at Chicago, and Chairman of the Cancer Prevention Coalition, warns us that there are more than eighty chemical components in today's cosmetics and household products which are cancer-causing agents. Cancers among men, women, and children are increasing at alarming rates. Millions of dollars are being poured into finding treatments, but curing cancer and other diseases is not possible unless we address the causes.

In his books, *The Safe Shopper's Bible, Unreasonable Risks,* and *Cancer-Gate: How to Win the Losing Cancer War,* Dr. Epstein lists products that contain undisclosed carcinogens and a wide range of other toxic ingredients. These "horrific substances," as he calls them, can be found in soaps, facial cleansers, deodorants, shaving creams, toothpastes, lotions, shampoos, conditioners, styling aids, blushes, eye shadows, mascara, perfumes, hair color, nail polish, nail polish remover, and aerosol hair sprays. The toxic substances in aerosol hair sprays, for example, are micro-minute and put you at risk for lung disease.

Also, animal parts are used in a lot of products that we aren't even aware of. Blood is used in nutritional food supplements, bones are used in desserts, intestines are used in detergents, and animal fats are used in soaps and lipsticks. We don't know about them because the ingredient lists are not obliged to spell out the sources.

Food irradiation is another hidden danger. Yes, it may be important for safety. However, it also kills important nutrition in food and leaves toxic by-products such as benzene and cyclobutanones, toxins which can cause genetic damage. About a year ago, I attended a press conference organized by the Cancer Prevention Coalition regarding the change of name from "food irradiation" to either "cold pasteurization" or "SureBeam." In attendance were scientists, medical doctors, various consumer protection groups, nuclear industry representatives, members of the Food and Drug Administration and the media. SureBeam had already been approved by the FDA, and needless to say there was strong opposition from the consumer protection groups, researchers, and the Cancer Prevention Coalition.

An Indian medical scientist, who studied food irradiation and its effects extensively, reported on a case study in which she gave under-nourished children (whose daily diet consisted of chapatti, an Indian flat bread), chapatti made with irradiated flour. She stopped the research after three weeks because these children's cell counts dropped so drastically.

Contrary to all the information and protests, the spokeswoman for the nuclear industry and FDA disregarded it all and proclaimed SureBeam's complete safety. SureBeam is now the official name and it is being proudly promoted as food safety, in fast food chains and grocery stores. The good news is that it is no longer allowed in school cafeterias, after an outcry from mothers.

It's a daunting picture. But we can start by educating ourselves, and boycotting products with labels we cannot read or understand. We can also make a big difference by buying certified organic/biodynamic products wherever possible. Organic certification is the only reassurance we have that we are not being poisoned by our purchases. The Organic Consumer Trade Association has done great work to set a precedent in the organic food movement with its certification. Yes, we pay more, because the Association is a private enterprise, and farmers, manufacturers, and restaurant owners have to pay to be certified, driving up the cost of the products. Hopefully in the future that will change. But in the meantime, it's worth paying for a reassurance that a product is free of poisons—not to mention the vastly greater nutritional value that organic produce has been scientifically shown to have.

We need to stop being naïve consumers. We are still being misled by cosmetics and household and other products that bear the label "natural." Anything that comes from the earth can be called "natural"—including petro-chemicals. As the word "organic" became popular, cosmetic and other consumer companies started taking advantage and using the term as a green-wash. The organic food movement trademarked "organic" to help consumer clarification with foods, but there is no current FDA ruling on cosmetic, household and other consumer products' organic labeling. Until the food law is applied to other domains these companies will continue to mislead consumers.

So we need to educate ourselves—and educate others. We can join or spearhead consumer activist groups, and lobby our politicians to fight for full disclosure of harmful ingredients on all consumer products. And we should remind ourselves every day that we live in a consumer democracy and we vote with what we buy. Let's vote wisely.

Eco-Chic

Fashion, today, is a multi-hundred-billion dollar industry, with hundreds of millions being spent on fashion magazines and advertising alone. The word *fashion* comes from the Latin word *factio*, the act of making or creating. It also means the prevailing style at a particular time. Fashion is a creative art and aesthetic expression that is applied to clothing, jewelry, cosmetics, furniture, industrial design, architecture, music, cars, etc. Fashion can make us feel good because it brings a sense of newness to the now and helps us to be noticed by others. It allows us to express our uniqueness as individuals. We can become victims of fashion or we can use fashion to make us feel better—especially if the fabrics and their microfibers are made from materials which are non-toxic and can be composted.

Fashion is what allowed me to create success in the cosmetic field. My main focus was to create pure, botanical-based personal care products, but the aesthetics of how they smelled, how they felt, even how the packaging looked, had to appeal to very fashionable women in salons and retail stores. I created a niche that I called "eco-chic" or "eco-hip" or "eco-intelligent."

Eco-chic today, however, is no longer a niche; I consider it the future of all fashion. If design pollutes, it should no longer be called fashion. Then it is a danger, and is no longer a form of creativity but a form of destruction.

Non-sustainable fashion destroys through the use of synthetic substances that pollute the earth and exploit our natural resources. It destroys by distributing particles of toxic substances to the people who use the fashions as well as to the people who make them. It destroys by harming and killing animals for skins, fur, and research, and it destroys by exploiting cheap labor in impoverished countries.

I am happy that there are now some major celebrities and fashion designers who are looking to eco-chic for a great opportunity. We'll see more and more celebrities going in this direction because they have the clout, the style, and the heart to make a difference. The new brand of eco-chic celebrities are looking for more than photo opportunities to make their presence felt; they are doing something to help relieve suffering and create a more humane, sustainable world.

There is now a great opportunity to look at fashion and design and give it some new relevance and honorable meaning, while creating abundant success. Let's make fashion part of the alivelihood paradigm. Saving the planet doesn't have to be a burden; it can be chic, creative and profitable.

SUSTAINABLE SUCCESS

My teacher Dr. Swami Rama always reminded me: "You are the architect of your life and you create your own destiny." In these pages, I have shared with you some of the building blocks I have used, and continue to use each day, in the architecture of my inner business, my relationships, my companies, and the future I want to create for our planet. They are simple principles, but fueled by intention, passion and love for all living things, they really can create miracles.

Once again, if we want not just to make a living, but to make alivelihood for our planet, we need to:

- Wake up to our inner dynamics and our interdependence with all living things
- Serve selflessly, seeing our customers as ourselves
- Visualize our goals and pursue them with positive discipline
- Turn every crisis into an opportunity
- Be a dedicated apprentice to great teachers and to life itself
- Tune our mind and senses through meditation to connect with the intelligence of nature
- Manage the laws of cause and effect in our own lives by conducting a daily in-ventory
- Ask ourselves: How can we serve, nurture and sustain the planet and its people in our business ventures?

- Educate ourselves, through study and direct experience, about the realities of our planetary crisis
- Learn to work and communicate as part of a dynamic team-system
- Clone ourselves through teaching others
- Create holistic business environments
- Make a business opportunity of the environmental crisis by designing innovative, sustainable products
- Vote wisely with what we buy
- Give thanks in our prayers for our successes — past, present and future
- Reinvent ourselves daily
- Forgive the cause of past and present painful experiences, unconditionally
- Remember gracefully our lessons — they are a gift of God

Imagine what could happen, for example, if the kind of energy that has created the internet revolution over the last ten years or the kind of creativity that drives the endless reinvention of popular culture was unleashed into sustainability. It's not far away. I believe it is the eco-preneurs and eco-consumers who will save the earth, because they will make it a great business opportunity and a great lifestyle. And that could be each and every one of us, because it's in our evolutionary blueprint. As the great Jesuit paleontologist Pierre Teilhard de Chardin wrote, "Someday, after mastering the winds, the waves, the tides and gravity, we shall harness for God the energies of love, and then, for a second time in the history of the world, man will have discovered fire."

ABOUT THE AUTHOR:
HORST M. RECHELBACHER

Horst M. Rechelbacher is an active environmentalist, innovative business leader, author and artist. He is the founder of the Aveda Corporation, a global plant-based cosmetic company, which he began in 1978. He has also founded Intelligent Nutrients, a biodynamic, organic functional foods and nutraceuticals corporation, and HMR Enterprises, which specializes in film, arts and antiques.

Born in Austria, the son of an herbalist and naturalist, Horst began a three-year apprenticeship in the beauty and salon industry at the age of fourteen. Since the mid-1960s he has specialized in analyzing the chemical constitution of plants while also pioneering the practical use of flower and plant-based flavor-aroma-therapy, functional foods and nutraceuticals for the benefit of personal health and well-being. In his continuing effort to study plant-based medicine, he has collaborated with noted physicians, chemists and pharmacognosists as well as experts and traditional healers throughout the world, especially in India and Asia, and with tribes in the Brazilian Rainforest and North America. Horst is the recipient of an *honoris causa* doctorate in Ayurveda from Gurukul Mahavidyalaya Twalapur, Haridwar University.

Horst was voted one of the most notable Austrians living in America by the Austrian press, along with Arnold Schwarzenegger and Wolfgang Puck. He was voted one of the most influential environmentalists in the US in 1995 and again in 2005, by *Vanity Fair* magazine. Horst is one of the three original founders of Business for Social Responsibility, which illustrates his belief that businesses not only have the responsibility but the greatest opportunity to provide sustainability to all living species. And in 2004, he was a founding member of the Organic Center for Education, Research and Promotion. Also in 2004, Horst was awarded the Lifetime Achievement Award from the beauty industry. He is an advisor and supporter of the Cancer Prevention Coalition and founder and chairman of the Horst M. Rechelbacher Foundation, a philanthropic organization dedicated to social and environmental preservation projects that operate on a grass-roots level.

Horst currently resides in Wisconsin and New York City. He continues to promote, through profit and non-profit organizations alike, sustainable development and constructive environmental practices.

Horst has authored two books, *Rejuvenation* and *Aveda Rituals*. He was also executive producer on *Hidden Medicine*, an independent film that premiered at the 1999 Sundance Film Festival.

VICTOR J. ZURBEL, CO-AUTHOR

Victor Zurbel is a former award-winning copywriter and art director for major advertising agencies, including the original, legendary Doyle Dane Bernbach. Currently, Victor is a writer and art director at the Peter Max Studio and has written, edited and designed several Peter Max art books. Victor is also in the process of creating a new media company, awaretv.com

ELLEN DALY, CO-AUTHOR

Ellen Daly has worked as an editor and writing consultant for the past ten years in book and magazine publishing in London and the US. She specializes in contemporary spirituality, business, and sustainability, and is an Associate Editor at *What Is Enlightenment?* magazine.

For further resources and more information on the art of sustainable success visit: www.alivelihood.com

Do You Love Me?

A lover asked his beloved,
Do you love yourself more
than you love me?

The beloved replied,
I have died to myself
and I live for you.

I've disappeared from myself
and my attributes.
I am present only for you.

I have forgotten all my learning,
but from knowing you
I have become a scholar.

I have lost all my strength,
but from your power
I am able.

If I love myself
I love you.
If I love you
I love myself.

Jalaluddin Rumi